40 days

Journal only

A 40 day meditation journal
for the beginner yogi
from a beginner Kundalini yogi.

40 days

Journal only

A 40 day meditation journal
for the beginner yogi
from a beginner Kundalini yogi.

by Paolla

First edition
December 2014

LM
Leslei Morgan Ltd
London, England

Published by **Leslei Morgan Ltd**

Copyright © 2014 **Leslei Morgan Ltd**
The moral right of the author, **Paolla Grecco**, has been asserted.
Book cover concept by **Paolla Grecco** and design by **Karyn Töws**
The author is grateful to quote from the following:

The Power of Compassion;
Copyright © His Holiness the XIV Dalai Lama 2001

Joseph Campbell and the Power of Myth will Bill Moyers;
courtesy of Apostrophe S Productions, Inc.

The Alchemist;
Copyright © Paulo Coelho and Alan R. Clarke 1992

Reaching ME in ME, Kundalini Yoga as Taught by Yogi Bhajan®;
Copyright © 2009 Kundalini Research Institute © 2000 Yogi Bhajan

Every effort has been made to contact the copyright holders.
The publisher will be glad to correct any errors or omissions in future
editions.

A CIP catalogue record for this book is available
from the British Library.
ISBN 978-0-9575341-7-9

First published in Great Britain in 2014 by

LESLEI
MORGAN

number 3 – 24 Ramsey Walk,
London, N1 2NH, United Kingdom
lesleimorgan@gmail.com

Please remember *this is my own journey* and it may not be anything like your journey with yoga.

This publication is not sold for profit but at cost. This is the **journal only** version for those solely interested in a tool to aid during meditation.

The other option to this title is the **journal and book** version which is presented into two parts: the first with 40 days' worth of structured journal pages for your own use and the second with 23 accompanying chapters where I share my personal experiences.

Any version of this title is only meant to serve as an inspiring tool for those beginning any form of targeted meditation.

This is not only for those practising Kundalini, although this was my meditative framework, and neither represents the views of any official organisations engaged in delivering kundalini yoga as taught by Yogi Bhajan.

Also note this is not presented as 'high-brow' reading or professional advice, but rather straight from my heart ♥

feedback is received via
40DaysMeditation@gmail.com
groups/40DaysMeditation
Please rate us on Amazon.

DEDICATION

For those
threading their
own beads
here I offer a few
of mine.

I've cried a lot yesterday
3x times for no reason, is hard
to evidence it, but the back pain
come on day 3 of my SAKti chanting
and on day 5 of SAKti I started
crying for no reason... and the
crying seemed to help relieve
the pain on the left of my back ribs.
This is powerful stuff; if I had not
done 2 decades of therapy I would
think it was due to some DIY, but
I learned in therapy that I project
a lot in my body, that is what
is unspoken and unresolved

PAUSE,

AND BREATH...

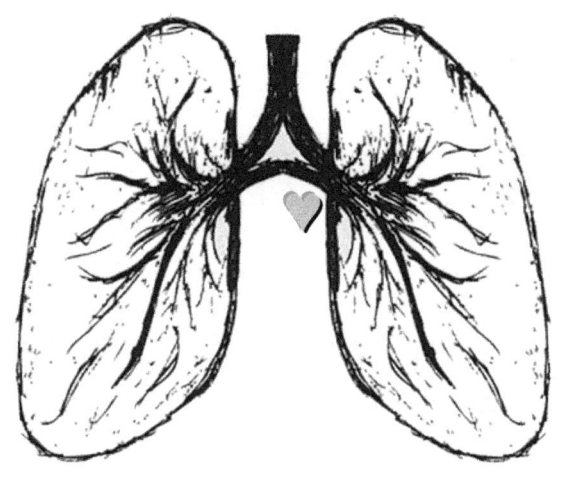

...DEEEEPLY

Journal's Contents

Extra Bits

40 days

Journal only

The hardest thing I had to deal with
was bringing the same discipline
I had in my professional life into my personal one.
For when the time came up I realised
I hadn't lived in my personal life
for many, many years.

INTRODUCTION
by Perla Aviram (Kirinpreet)

Sat Nam

As I write this introduction I am reminded of a quote by Yogi Bhajan, who brought Kundalini Yoga to the west and whose teachings I have been experiencing and teaching for the past 6 years:

"If you want to learn something, read about it.
If you want to understand something, write about it.
If you want to master something, teach it."

What a perfect example. The unfolding of Paolla's journey begins with her own experience, which she journals regularly in order to process and understand. I was lucky enough to see her throughout the unfolding of this project. I have watched her begin to experience things more deeply, interpret things more openly, accept things more calmly. Most importantly she began to remember with greater clarity who she is and where her truth lies. Today her experiences are turned into a tool to

3

help guide others on their journey, a brave and important step on the way to mastery! I am extremely happy to be contributing to this tool and believe that it will be of great use to her and many others.

So what is Kundalini Yoga?

Kundalini Yoga is the Yoga of awareness. A Raj, (Royal), Yoga which was kept secret for many years and taught only to kings or priests or those who were found 'worthy' of it'. Why is it a royal yoga? Why was it kept secret? Because it puts us, human beings, on the throne; awakening us to realise that nothing is outside of us; sensitising us to notice that we are far more than the limitations offered by the experiences of our mind or physical body. There is universal energy running through and around us. This energy is part of us and is as much a resource in this life as are the physical body and mind. All we need to do is tap into it. Kundalini Yoga awakens you to reconnect to the true and infinite you, pure consciousness, able to direct energy, the driving force for all life and manifestation of all things. Recognizing this brings great freedom yet comes with great responsibility.

Kundalini Yoga, as taught by Yogi Bhajan, is a safe and powerful practice. No special initiation is needed and anyone, at all levels of experience can work to achieve rapid and effective change.

In Kundalini Yoga we work with 'Kriyas' rather than individual postures. Kriya means complete action, an action that leads to a set result or manifestation. So in our Yoga this means we work with sequences of breath, postures and sound current which together bring on a particular state. The effect of the Kriya is so much bigger than the sum of its parts. Its perfection comes together within the flow of the whole and that is why the Kriyas are never changed or tampered with. You cannot pick and choose parts of the Kriya. All Kriyas are practiced and delivered just as they were handed down, for thousands and thousands of years – and there are thousands of these to choose from! When you master a particular Kriya you master a particular aspect of your awareness. Discipline is a very important part of achieving that.

How do you master a Kriya? You practice it daily for 40 days (at least). 40 days is what it takes to change a habit. Most of the time we operate from automatic patterns we are not even aware, such as emotions and responses relating to past experiences. These patterns can be broken, giving us the freedom and joy to be in every moment and choose our response. It is hard to grasp it but try and imagine how wonderful that could feel! Being present, riding the wave of life with joy and curiosity meeting every new challenge with an open heart and finding creative ways to delve into it. Instead what do we do? We analyse, prepare, fear, predict and we react emotionally thus creating disappointment, anxiety and resistance to the natural flow.

Yogis in general call the daily spiritual practice 'Sadhana' and this is best practiced early in the morning before sunrise. These hours are more conducive to achieving a meditative state. The mind is calmer, the world is less active and if you do your practice before the start of your day, you set yourself to be more centred, clear and radiant for the rest of it.

We are blessed to be living in a time of great change, an astrological shift, a change in the electromagnetic field of the planet, a new age of consciousness, the age of Aquarius. For this special time Yogi Bhajan recommended for Kundalini students a 2.5 hour Sadhana to help maintain one's balance and identity during challenging times of change. The practice opens with recitation of the 'Japji', an universal prayer given by Guru Nanak the first Sikh Guru. It is considered the song of the soul and holds a very transformative sound current. There are 40 verses to the Japji, each offering a path to healing a particular aspect in life so although it is recommended to chant all verses in the morning, each verse can also be chanted and meditated upon individually.

Recitation of the Japji takes 20 minutes and typically the next part of a Kundalini Sadhana consists of a Kundalini Yoga Kriya, followed by approximately 10 minutes of deep relaxation and then 62 minutes of chanting. At the end of the 2.5 hours the sun would have risen and you will be vibrating a different current, ready for whatever the day brings.

You must be thinking there is no chance anyone can stick to that! Well, the beauty of Sadhana is that it does not matter how long or how short a time you have, just do it. Any time you invest will be rewarded threefold or even tenfold if you allow it. If five minutes a day is all you have, Kundalini Yoga offers meditations and Kriyas which can be practiced for as little as three minutes a day and still have a powerful affect. You will discover, however that once you progress you will begin to find the time to do more.

Sadhana can be practiced alone or in a group. I truly recommend attending group Sadhanas as vibrations are raised and the heart really opens when such a powerful practice is shared.

So... do you need to be 'flexible', 'fit', 'spiritual', have a strong core etc. etc. etc. to practice Kundalini Yoga? The answer is No. Flexibility and physical strength will come but they are just the by-products. What is really important to explore during your practice is the true you and your own resources as they are. Your mind and body are such magnificent tools which are there to serve you, one just needs to accept and recognise it. During a difficult physical posture, be assured that your resources are much more than your muscles. If you rely only on them you are most likely to contract many additional unnecessary muscles leading to pain and difficulty. If you let go of as many muscles as possible, stay neutral and bring in breath and energy from deep within, you will master the posture much quicker and discover an altered state of consciousness too! Kundalini Yoga Kriyas are like life, once you discover how to bring everything into flow it does not really matter what the challenge is, a tough posture, a deadline at work or a difficult relationship. Do not hold on to your usual responses, do not give in to the suffering the mind creates. These are mechanisms that may have protected you in the past but they do not define you. The only way to move forward is by letting go, take another breath, open your heart to the challenge and let yourself cross that protective 'giving up point'. Beautiful things await on the other side.

Wishing you a wonderful journey.

Wahe Guru

Perla Aviram (Kirinpreet)

AUTHOR'S NOTE

As I started my own journal in preparation for the Kundalini discipline I delved into between 2013 and 2014, I realised I wished that a diary with a tailored structured existed rather than blank lines below a date. A journal where as I turned the pages I could easily see the gaps, low periods, important events or discoveries about myself. So on the eleventh of November 2013 I started writing this introduction as a means to manifest what it felt like a wonderful way to give back to others developing themselves through any form of yoga or spiritual practice.

As I now prepare for it to be published exactly 1 year after I started practicing 40 day meditation sets I would like to thank the invisible which keeps us alive, hopeful and healthy.

In practicing 3-11 minutes sets of 40 day meditation back-to-back over a period of 12 months, I stopped caring about dogmas or which way was the better teaching to follow. What I cared was that 40 day Kundalini meditations worked and that I was able to reconnect with the 'invisible' without losing my love for science and logic.

I also added to the journaling structure some tracking grids, as I found during my 20 years battling depression through conventional therapy, writing things down and tracking them was a good way to gain perspective. These fixed tracking grids allow you to grade your sleep, physical pains and enthusiasm, in addition there are blank ones for tracking whatever else you feel is of relevance to you.

There are many scientific or more 'credible books' about journaling, meditation or yoga than this one, yet I am not looking for credibility. I simply found myself with the means to offer others a tool which was not available to me in the form of this structured journal accompanied by a book with my own experiences and journal entries.

Whilst, writing this note I also cannot help but wonder if a person from 60-80 years ago travelled to our present, what would be his or her quality of interaction with us? I believe it would be excellent. I say this because during these past decades we have for one reason or another lost the ability to focus, to leave the house knowing exactly what we are set-out to do in that particular day. I reckon this time traveller would be able to manipulate a 'modern-day' person so easily. This is because we now leave home only knowing enough to get to the next point of the day, lending all our capability and focus to 24/7 electronic devices, push-emails, instant notifications and text.

I do love technology and wish all of it had been available to me when I was 12 years of age. But as a child learns that too much sugar leads to a tummy ache, I personally learnt that constant interruption of technology weakened my ability to focus. Thus weakening the ability to prevail through challenging periods or to simply be able to fully enjoy the good times. In this sense '40 days' is not only about helping you with journaling during a targeted yoga practice, hopefully it will also maximise your focus for a period of time. An enhanced focus helps identify aspects of your personal life you wish to address, or in my case which I have overlooked.

After this idea had sprung in my heart, I naturally criticised it, by thinking this would be a more genuine tool if it actually came out a year after completing teacher training or if I got some sort of official endorsement. But then my re-connected Self reminded me that the beauty I enjoy most in life is in spontaneity, an act of innocence and sincerity which we all could use a little bit more.

Thus, this journal comes out as it was conceived, by a beginner yogi about to turn-up the volume on her own journey, which brings all that is 'uncertain'.

If this first edition helps you organise your thoughts and emotions in a useful manner as well as being the companion I wish I had at the start of my own 40 day journey, then I have accomplished what I was set out to do in the first place.

As you read through this journal you may encounter terms you are not familiar with, in this case please refer to the **Factoids** chapter at the end with general definitions for certain terms. Also there is another chapter at the end called **Favourite Meditations**, in which I talk about some of my favourite sets and its original sources.

May the long-time sun shine upon you.

Paolla ♥

DAY SAMPLE

My intention is…

to have no fear.

Day Sample

	1	2	3	4	5
Sleep			✗		
Physical pains		✗	✗		
Enthusiasm			✗		
tongue				✗	
Skin				✗	
JUNK FOOD	nil ☺				

Focus	9 hrs chopped (3 & 6) slept late
Food eaten before bed	small portion of pasta, rice crispies
Today's to-dos	−DIY home − New year's plan − RUN − emails

Dreams:

had many, but couldn't
remember one clearly.

20

Day Sample

Thi journaling framework seems to become more and more important, and it reminds me of a short fiction workshop we managed to write creative pieces with the time limit of 5 minutes by using a framework. It is beautiful when I am able to contain the creative energy and manifest it ☺

I managed to contain my cravings for starch and refined sugar a bit better, the framework was to drink a large glass of water and wait to see if it was hunger or just a craving... but rice crispy last night was inevitable. I made them from scratch ☺😋

Impressions:

√ Read Japji portion 11x at 2am

Pains

L / R

according to Ostheo is just on the line of the Sympatico System of nerves responsible for "fight or flight" aka stress.

tongue

L / R

LIVER   SPLEEN

REVISED
ACOPUNTURE
NUTRITIONAL
LIST.

Feeling Stuck

Upper back

-try running
-go to Ostheo
to release
"Sympatico".

Your intention is...

_____

Day 1 to 7

'... feeling ill in my gut, I know why
and on top of it I carry some juvenile
guilt in writing an email to the office
that I will not come in, where does
this guilty feeling comes from?
Then I follow Rook to the living
room where once again he sits on
my mat as if saying "can I be
more obvious?" Is 4:30am now,
then I remember dreaming with
him... but before I give in to
his tender look I make myself in
the mood to meditate... I light
a candle, boil the tea and bathe
in cold water, my feet that is, small
gentle gestures which felt amazing...'

Day 1

	1	2	3	4	5
Sleep					
Physical pains					
Enthusiasm					

Focus	
Food eaten before bed	
Today's to-dos	

Dreams:

_____

_____

_____

_____

_____

_____

_____

_____

_____

_____

_____

Impressions:

Journaling:

Day 2

	1	2	3	4	5
Sleep					
Physical pains					
Enthusiasm					

Focus	
Food eaten before bed	
Today's to-dos	

Dreams:

_____

_____

_____

_____

_____

_____

_____

_____

_____

_____

Impressions:

Journaling:

Day 3

	1	2	3	4	5
Sleep					
Physical pains					
Enthusiasm					

Focus	
Food eaten before bed	
Today's to-dos	

Dreams:

Impressions:

Journaling:

Day 4

	1	2	3	4	5
Sleep					
Physical pains					
Enthusiasm					

Focus	
Food eaten before bed	
Today's to-dos	

Dreams:

Impressions:

Journaling:

Day 5

	1	2	3	4	5
Sleep					
Physical pains					
Enthusiasm					

Focus	
Food eaten before bed	
Today's to-dos	

Dreams:

_____

_____

_____

_____

_____

_____

_____

_____

_____

_____

_____

Impressions:

Journaling:

Day 6

	1	2	3	4	5
Sleep					
Physical pains					
Enthusiasm					

Focus	
Food eaten before bed	
Today's to-dos	

Dreams:

_____

_____

_____

_____

_____

_____

_____

_____

_____

_____

_____

Impressions:

Journaling:

Day 7

	1	2	3	4	5
Sleep					
Physical pains					
Enthusiasm					

Focus	
Food eaten before bed	
Today's to-dos	

Dreams:

Impressions:

Journaling:

weekly review

Week 1

In your own words:

Day 8 to 14

'... today feels incredibly wonderful, I only slept four hours but when I did the 'burn anger' meditation for two minutes it felt like a mere second. There is so much energy. Now I understand what Paulo Coelho means by knowing when you are filled with enthusiasm from doing what you love. Yesterday I spent 4 hours doing something I've never done before but which felt right and today feels like I could run that marathon in just 3 hours...'

Day 8

	1	2	3	4	5
Sleep					
Physical pains					
Enthusiasm					

Focus	
Food eaten before bed	
Today's to-dos	

Dreams:

_____

_____

_____

_____

_____

_____

_____

_____

_____

_____

Impressions:

Journaling:

Day 9

	1	2	3	4	5
Sleep					
Physical pains					
Enthusiasm					

Focus	
Food eaten before bed	
Today's to-dos	

Dreams:

_____

_____

_____

_____

_____

_____

_____

_____

_____

_____

Impressions:

Journaling:

Day 10

	1	2	3	4	5
Sleep					
Physical pains					
Enthusiasm					

Focus	
Food eaten before bed	
Today's to-dos	

Dreams:

_____

_____

_____

_____

_____

_____

_____

_____

_____

_____

Impressions:

Journaling:

Day 11

	1	2	3	4	5
Sleep					
Physical pains					
Enthusiasm					

Focus	
Food eaten before bed	
Today's to-dos	

Dreams:

Impressions:

Journaling:

Day 12

	1	2	3	4	5
Sleep					
Physical pains					
Enthusiasm					

Focus	
Food eaten before bed	
Today's to-dos	

Dreams:

Impressions:

Journaling:

Day 13

	1	2	3	4	5
Sleep					
Physical pains					
Enthusiasm					

Focus	
Food eaten before bed	
Today's to-dos	

Dreams:

Impressions:

Journaling:

Day 14

	1	2	3	4	5
Sleep					
Physical pains					
Enthusiasm					

Focus	
Food eaten before bed	
Today's to-dos	

Dreams:

Impressions:

Journaling:

weekly review

Week 2

In your own words:

Day 15 to 21

Day 15

	1	2	3	4	5
Sleep					
Physical pains					
Enthusiasm					

Focus	
Food eaten before bed	
Today's to-dos	

Dreams:

Impressions:

Journaling:

Day 16

	1	2	3	4	5
Sleep					
Physical pains					
Enthusiasm					

Focus	
Food eaten before bed	
Today's to-dos	

Dreams:

Impressions:

Journaling:

Day 17

	1	2	3	4	5
Sleep					
Physical pains					
Enthusiasm					

Focus	
Food eaten before bed	
Today's to-dos	

Dreams:

_____

_____

_____

_____

_____

_____

_____

_____

_____

_____

_____

Impressions:

Journaling:

Day 18

	1	2	3	4	5
Sleep					
Physical pains					
Enthusiasm					

Focus	
Food eaten before bed	
Today's to-dos	

Dreams:

Impressions:

Journaling:

Day 19

	1	2	3	4	5
Sleep					
Physical pains					
Enthusiasm					

Focus	
Food eaten before bed	
Today's to-dos	

Dreams:

Impressions:

Journaling:

Day 20

	1	2	3	4	5
Sleep					
Physical pains					
Enthusiasm					

Focus	
Food eaten before bed	
Today's to-dos	

Dreams:

_____

_____

_____

_____

_____

_____

_____

_____

_____

_____

Impressions:

Journaling:

Day 21

	1	2	3	4	5
Sleep					
Physical pains					
Enthusiasm					

Focus	
Food eaten before bed	
Today's to-dos	

Dreams:

Impressions:

Journaling:

weekly review

Week 3

In your own words:

Day 22 to 28

"…go to the edge of the cliff and jump off. Build your wings on the way down…"

~Ray Bradbury,

Brown Daily Herald, Mar. 24, 1995

Day 22

	1	2	3	4	5
Sleep					
Physical pains					
Enthusiasm					

Focus	
Food eaten before bed	
Today's to-dos	

Dreams:

Impressions:

Journaling:

Day 23

	1	2	3	4	5
Sleep					
Physical pains					
Enthusiasm					

Focus	
Food eaten before bed	
Today's to-dos	

Dreams:

Impressions:

Journaling:

Day 24

	1	2	3	4	5
Sleep					
Physical pains					
Enthusiasm					

Focus	
Food eaten before bed	
Today's to-dos	

Dreams:

Impressions:

Journaling:

Day 25

	1	2	3	4	5
Sleep					
Physical pains					
Enthusiasm					

Focus	
Food eaten before bed	
Today's to-dos	

Dreams:

Impressions:

Journaling:

Day 26

	1	2	3	4	5
Sleep					
Physical pains					
Enthusiasm					

Focus	
Food eaten before bed	
Today's to-dos	

Dreams:

Impressions:

Journaling:

Day 27

	1	2	3	4	5
Sleep					
Physical pains					
Enthusiasm					

Focus	
Food eaten before bed	
Today's to-dos	

Dreams:

Impressions:

Journaling:

Day 28

	1	2	3	4	5
Sleep					
Physical pains					
Enthusiasm					

Focus	
Food eaten before bed	
Today's to-dos	

Dreams:

_____

_____

_____

_____

_____

_____

_____

_____

_____

_____

Impressions:

Journaling:

weekly review

Week 4

In your own words:

Day 29 to 35

©1999, Michael Dougan

Day 29

	1	2	3	4	5
Sleep					
Physical pains					
Enthusiasm					

Focus	
Food eaten before bed	
Today's to-dos	

Dreams:
_____
_____
_____
_____
_____
_____
_____
_____
_____
_____
_____

Impressions:

Journaling:

Day 30

	1	2	3	4	5
Sleep					
Physical pains					
Enthusiasm					

Focus	
Food eaten before bed	
Today's to-dos	

Dreams:

Impressions:

Journaling:

Day 31

	1	2	3	4	5
Sleep					
Physical pains					
Enthusiasm					

Focus	
Food eaten before bed	
Today's to-dos	

Dreams:

Impressions:

Journaling:

Day 32

	1	2	3	4	5
Sleep					
Physical pains					
Enthusiasm					

Focus	
Food eaten before bed	
Today's to-dos	

Dreams:

Impressions:

Journaling:

Day 33

	1	2	3	4	5
Sleep					
Physical pains					
Enthusiasm					

Focus	
Food eaten before bed	
Today's to-dos	

Dreams:

Impressions:

Journaling:

Day 34

	1	2	3	4	5
Sleep					
Physical pains					
Enthusiasm					

Focus	
Food eaten before bed	
Today's to-dos	

Dreams:

Impressions:

Journaling:

Day 35

	1	2	3	4	5
Sleep					
Physical pains					
Enthusiasm					

Focus	
Food eaten before bed	
Today's to-dos	

Dreams:
_____
_____
_____
_____
_____
_____
_____
_____
_____
_____
_____

Impressions:

Journaling:

weekly review

Week 5

In your own words:

Day 36 to 40

'You already have
everything you need.'
~ Unknown

Day 36

	1	2	3	4	5
Sleep					
Physical pains					
Enthusiasm					

Focus	
Food eaten before bed	
Today's to-dos	

Dreams:

Impressions:

Journaling:

Day 37

	1	2	3	4	5
Sleep					
Physical pains					
Enthusiasm					

Focus	
Food eaten before bed	
Today's to-dos	

Dreams:

Impressions:

Journaling:

Day 38

	1	2	3	4	5
Sleep					
Physical pains					
Enthusiasm					

Focus	
Food eaten before bed	
Today's to-dos	

Dreams:

Impressions:

Journaling:

Day 39

	1	2	3	4	5
Sleep					
Physical pains					
Enthusiasm					

Focus	
Food eaten before bed	
Today's to-dos	

Dreams:

Impressions:

Journaling:

Day 40

	1	2	3	4	5
Sleep					
Physical pains					
Enthusiasm					

Focus	
Food eaten before bed	
Today's to-dos	

Dreams:

Impressions:

Journaling:

weekly review

Week 6

In your own words:

THE 40TH DAY

There were many 40 day meditations that I followed in the last 12 months, ranging from the ability to communicate by focusing on the throat *chakra*, 'reconnect with the feminine', 'chase away shadows', become fearless and to 'burn anger'.

Today is the 40th day of 'healing a broken heart' meditation, it is a sad day, which intuitively coincided with many things. It was Summer Equinox a moment of transition in nature and also the weekend I completely re-arranged the flat. Physically moving things around always helped me mark the start of something new. In other words this 40th day was a perfect moment for letting go of my room for the Summer to welcome friends and family into my home.

Letting go of the room where my little family of three grew, myself and two beautiful adopted kittens Luna and Cook, it was tough. This was difficult because a few months earlier Luna moved into another realm after a tragic accident at home and because she melted my heart during the nine months we spent together.

That room held so much love, it was where I

unexpectedly opened my heart *chakra* in a 'burn anger' meditation, experiencing the true power within us. This experience lasted for days, followed by one of the few times, in my forty years in this planet, that I fell into a completely restful and safe sleep.

The room where Cook, my tabby ball of love, competed for space over my chest and neck during the many curled up mornings they nursed me with little heart beats of joy. Then unexpectedly is also Luna's last resting place after discovering her body inside the washing machine as an emptied a load at 3am.

This 40th day was a Wednesday, it was an important day, a Wednesday of interrupted plans. It was also the 40th day after *White Tantric Yoga*, it was also exactly one month before Luna's and Cook's one year birthday. It was the day I understood what really mattered to me in this world. And whatever this 40th day may come to mean for you I truly wish it may come from your true heart and take you where you need to be.

PRESSING PRINT

To come from a personal journey to actually publish this guided journal was easy and it was hard. It was easy because I did not have to think about it, it is what they say 'it wrote itself' and it also helped that I had already self-published before. However, it was hard in the sense that I had to transcribe my own journal and research through the many entries for what would be meaningful. Admittedly every time I tried to do this I was lost in tears and that awful feeling of re-living your struggles and doubts.

In order to press print I have reached out to many people, including a *reiki* and heart energy practitioner, acupuncturists, blend diets, G-d, the blessings of Glastonbury's White Spring waters and a medium.

Finally lost in an angst almost turned into depression I read from a Paulo Coelho's quote on Facebook what I needed to hear.

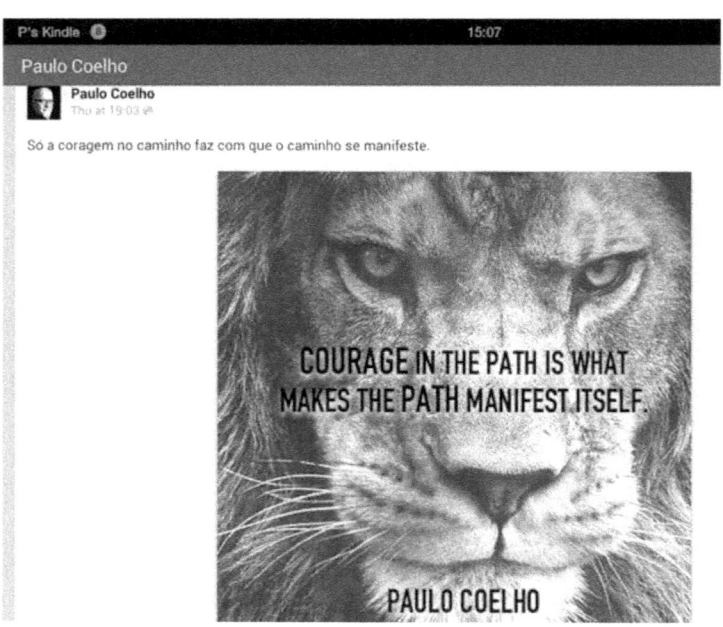

Paulo Coelho
Thu at 19:03

Só a coragem no caminho faz com que o caminho se manifeste.

COURAGE IN THE PATH IS WHAT MAKES THE PATH MANIFEST ITSELF.

PAULO COELHO

Reading that and giving in to three days of comfort food to numb myself so I could read through my own entries did it. It was hard, but it worked., so I truly hope it helps you.

Finally, in my own adaptation of one of my favourite Kundalini adapted songs, I wish you that...

'May the long-time sun shine upon you,

all love surround you

and the pure light within you,

guide your way *home*.'

FAVOURITE MEDITATIONS

Here is a succinct list of my favourite kundalini *mantras* (chanting/praying), *mudras* (hand positions) and Kriyas (sets of exercise as taught by Yogi Bhajan).

On a personal note, I do not believe if you use the same meditations I did this will yield the same results. However, I do believe that sharing the tools I used in my journey may inspire you in yours.

For the readers practising Kundalini Kriyas or using the Sikh *mantras,* it is taught that you tune in first. Tuning in means opening with a specific *mantra*. In many yoga classes of the Buddhist tradition this tuning in is chanting OM three times at the start and end of a class. In Kundalini one typically starts with 'Ong Namo, Guru Dev Namo' three times and may close with a variety of *mantras*. But is important with the Kundalini practise to tuning with the *Ong Namo*.

Another aspect of practising most types of yoga is to rest after the exercise even a meditation. In Kundalini this is also taught with an emphasis on 'grounding' your body be it with a cup of tea or a snack at the end.

When I used *mantras* for my morning meditations I

was asked to repeat them at least eleven times. When I used poses, movement and breathing I was always asked to do it at least 3 minutes to a maximum of 11 minutes. In reality there were only two sets I was able to have a constant commitment to the 11 minutes. This is because when you reach that point of shift, which is often emotional at first, coming to the mat to just chant a few lines eleven times can feel scarily powerful. On those days I could not make it to the mat, I laid or sat in bed, visualising that I did it, and in my heart I know I did.

Above all… always have fun!

Official sources for detailed teachings
for Yogi Bhajan's Kundalini yoga

www.kundaliniresearchinstitute.org

www.libraryofteachings.com

'Reaching ME in me'

Kundalini Yoga as Taught by Yogi Bhajan®

Published by Kundalini Research Institute

Alternative sources for content

www.spiritvoyage.com

www.pinklotus.org

MANTRAS

Please consult the relevant official websites and publications for further details of using mantras in conjunction with Kundalini mediations as taught by Yogi Bhajan.

'ONG NAMO, GURU DEV NAMO'

This is from Sanskrit, and apparently it seems to be a deviation from the grammatically correct version 'Om gurudevaya namaha' this *Adi Mantra* is always chanted at the beginning of any Kundalini Yoga practice. This serves as a tool to tuning one with their higher self. Ong is 'Infinite Creative energy in manifestation and activity'. ('Om' or Aum is God absolute and un-manifested), Namo is 'reverent greetings' implying humility, Guru means 'teacher or wisdom', Dev means "Divine or of God" and Namo reaffirms humility and reverence. In all it means, "I call upon Divine Wisdom".

Source: http://www.kundaliniyoga.org/mantra.html

'HUMMEE HUM BRAHM HUM'

Purpose: This *mantra* is like a harmonious cord of energetic gestures of sound which increases in us the sensitivity to feel alive and to live completely.

Meaning: We are we, We are GOD/infinity

(G-O-D = the Generating Organizing Destroying/Delivering force within every one of us)

This is a perfect *mantra* for expanding the heart Centre and sense of self.

Humee Hum = Earth energy. We are we

It is the sense of self we get when connecting with people or with things, with all of that we are part of. We become truly ourselves as we feel our connection with everything.

Brahm Hum = The heavens, ether, subtle, celestial part of ourselves.

We are god/ Brahm/ Creative infinity. The formless creative witness that is within us. Together they are like a heart Beat: Humme Hum Brahm Hum

Note: There are various ways to use this mantra.

'CHATTR CHAKRKR VARTEE'

This mantra is referred to as the last four lines of the sacred Sikh prayer called Japji Sahib.

Purpose: it recommended to me for letting go of fears.

Meaning:

Chattr chakrkr vartee
Thou art pervading in all the four quarters of the universe

Chattr chakrkr bhugatay
Thou are the enjoyer in all the four quarters of the universe

Suyumbhav subhang sarab daa sarab jugatay
Thou art self-illuminated and united with all

Dukaalang pranaasee dayaalang saroopay,
Destroyer of bad times embodiment of mercy

Sadaa ung sungay abhangang bibhootay
Thou art the everlasting giver of indestructible power

Note: recommended to me that these lines be recited eleven times.

Source: 'Reaching ME in me', Published by Kundalini Research Institute.

'ADI SHAKTI'

Purpose: to tune in with the **Divine Mother**, generating energy. Chanting it eliminates fears and fulfils desires. Adi Shakti means the "Primal Power," Sarab Shakti means "All Power", and Prithum Bhagawati means "which creates through God."

Meaning:

Aadee Shaktee, Namo, Namo,
I bow to (or call on) the primal power.

Sarab shaktee, Namo, Namo,
I bow to (or call on) the all-encompassing power and energy.

Prithum Bhaagavatee, Namo, Namo,
I bow to (or call on) that through which God creates
.
Kundalinee, Maataa Shaktee, Namo, Namo
I bow to (or call on) the creative power of the Kundalini, the Divine Mother Power.

Adi Shakti, is also a Sikh *mantra* which is part of the Japji Sahib, the sacred hymn composed by Guru Nanak Dev Ji.

Note: recommend to me to just sit in a quiet place and chant it daily 6-11 minutes, depending on how much time I had. Also to download a track to get used to the words, such as by Snatam Kaur.

Source: in accordance with KRI's International Kundalini Yoga, Teacher Training, Textbook, Level One, Instructor; Copyright 1969-2005.

ASANKH MURAKH ANDH GHOR.

Purpose: To chase away 'shadows', 'ghosts' of the past, madness and self-destructive behaviour.

Meaning:

Asankh murak andh ghor. Asankh chor haraam-khor
Countless fools in darkness extreme. Countless thieves do other's relieve

Asank paapi paa kar jaah. Asankh kuriar kure phiraah.
Countless sinners do sin incur. Countless liars in lies besmirch

Asankh malechh mal bhakhi khaah. Asankh nindak sir karah bhaar.
Countless the filthy in filth stay. Countless slanderers carry sway.

Naanak nich kahai vichaar. Vaariaa na jaavaa ek vaar.
Nanak lowly does a thought recall. Not enough sacrifice for once at call.

Jo tudh bhaavai saai bhali kaar. Tu sadaa salaamat Nirankar.
What pleaseth Tee is good for all. Thou abide ever the invisible lord.

Note: Again it was just recommended to me to recite it eleven times.

Source: Jap Ji by Man Mohan Singh.
Part of the sacred Japji Sahib Sikh hymn, verse 18th.

There is more about it you can find on the following link:

http://www.spiritvoyage.com/blog/index.php/mantra-for-sanity-asankh-murakh-the-18th-pauri-of-japji/

I often, keep it simple and concentrate on the vibration of the words which is what I enjoy the most. This is because personally when I attach meaning to the words is like an entire narrative turns on in my head, whereas when I only have the intention behind it I am able to silence any unnecessary dialogue a lot faster and enjoy the vibration and energy it activates.

KUNDALINI KRIYAS

Please consult the relevant official websites and publications for further details of executing any kundalini kriyas as taught by Yogi Bhajan.

CONQUER INNER ANGER AND BURN IT OUT
Reaching ME in me',
Published by Kundalini Research Institute
As originally taught by Yogi Bhajan, March 8, 1999

This is still one of the most powerful meditations to me,

Journal entry: '... This Friday was the 6th day of my 40 day dynamic meditation using the 'conquer inner anger and burn it out' Kriya from one on of the booklets I bought from an i-Sky booth at a yoga show.

I almost did not make it today, was good that this particular one is just one position for 11 minutes and it can be done either in the morning or in the evening. It was also challenging because at the same time I cut out added sugars or replacements from my diet for the duration of the 40 days - and everything has added sugar, it is insane. But as Paulo Coelho wrote in the Alchemist '...when you want something, all the universe conspires in helping you to achieve it...'

So tonight as I left yoga at Sadhaka by 8pm in Camden, still determined to burn all this extra energy which seems to release so intensely after I start any 40 day set, I headed off to Green Note on Parkway, Camden for an evening of folk/country with Toy Hearts, and it was bliss. As I was thirsty and hungry I approached the bar dreading all I could order at a pub in Camden with no sugar would be water, but to my surprise I had a fresh squeezed Orange juice with Samosas. Thank you, Universe...'

SAT KRIYA

Another one of my top favourites and apparently also Demi Moore's. The thing which will bother you the most is keeping the shoulders down.

The trick for me was to start mindfully keeping my chin tucked in. This helped me with posture. Once I felt comfortable with that I tried to find how to hold my arms without 'using my shoulders'. For me what helped was remember of this muscle underneath your arm pits (Teres Major), is the same I used to exercise a lot as a ballerina when holding my arms in first position.

Then it worked, those muscles became more 'aware' and easier to 'turn on' with time. After that your arms are just light as feather and you come to enjoy the beautiful balance of the position. I did it from 3 to 11 minutes, my favourite time was on a busy day at work, I cycled to a pop-up yoga by Borough Market to find out it was no longer. Frustrated but not defeated I found a less busy spot and sat in the sun and did my Sat Kriya quietly whilst I am sure I ended up on some tourist social page on the net. ☺

GRIEF RELEASE AND
TO HEAL A BROKEN HEART

This simple crossed legged meditation with hands on the heart was given to me to help me get through the loss of Luna, one of my kittens.

It was a beautiful and gentle meditation which of all the ones I practice outdoors in nature, is the least embarrassing. Often I went to the Inner Temple Gardens for this one and highly recommended it to be done in nature if possible.

CHRIST MUDRA
and Affirmation

'I am not my body, I am not my mind, I am not my spirit**, I am** the breath of G-d, **the breath of life,** the breath of life, the breath of G-d.'

I found this in one of my random online searches. It was another easy one to do for 11 minutes, and in reality I used a combination of the May and June videos by Nivair on YouTube, which made for a wonderful mediation.

I highly recommend watching his video. Once I even managed to squeeze a 5 min meditation on board of a sleeper coach from London to Edinburgh. The position itself was easy, but what stuck for me was the affirmation in English, which is not often something I choose.

The affirmation helped me avoid drifting out of the breathing. I mixed the affirmation with the Christ Mudra, palm down at heart centre below, minus the mantra of course as I was doing the breath of fire already. Although at advanced stages of breathing I found that I could do it all: pump my naval, sing and repeat the affirmation in my mind at the same time. But that is another book alone in itself.

GRAPHS

Sleep

Physical pains

Enthusiasm

5			
4			
3			
2			
1			

1 2 3 4 5 6 7 8 9 10 11 12 13 14 15 16 17 18 19 20 21 22 23 24 25 26 27 28 29 30 31 32 33 34 35 36 37 38 39 40

5			
4			
3			
2			
1			

1 2 3 4 5 6 7 8 9 10 11 12 13 14 15 16 17 18 19 20 21 22 23 24 25 26 27 28 29 30 31 32 33 34 35 36 37 38 39 40

5			
4			
3			
2			
1			

1 2 3 4 5 6 7 8 9 10 11 12 13 14 15 16 17 18 19 20 21 22 23 24 25 26 27 28 29 30 31 32 33 34 35 36 37 38 39 40

FACTOIDS

A

Adi Mantra: first call, often meaning the first morning prayer during the practice of Sadhana. In this publication is particular to the Japji Sahib, a Sikh sacred hymn, recited in kundalini Sadhana practices.

Asana: Sanskrit term used in yoga to refer to physical positions a yogi practises as exercises, these asanas or positions can be static or fluid in movement.

B

Breath of fire: Breath of fire looks like panting, but in fact is a much more sophisticated tool. At the start I was taught to put my hand on my belly and feeling the belly button or naval area suck in strongly whilst I exhaled. In time you focus on the exhale and the inhale happens naturally.

C

Chakras: in this publication is generally referred to the 8 chakras in Kundalini yoga, which are seen as ethereal points of energy with specific functions.

First Chakra: Security and Survival (red)
Location: End of the spine between the anus and sexual organs.

Second Chakra: Creativity (orange)
Location: Sex organs.

Third Chakra: Action and Balance (yellow)
Location: Area of the Navel Point, solar plexus.

Fourth Chakra: Love and Compassion (green)
Location: Middle of the chest on the breast bone at the level of the nipples.

Fifth Chakra: Projective Power of the Word (light blue)
Location: The throat.

Sixth Chakra: Intuition, Wisdom, and Identity (dark blue)
Location: Between the eyebrows (the "Third Eye").

Seventh (Crown) Chakra: Humility (violet)
Location: Crown of the head.

Eighth Chakra: The Aura (white)
Location: Electromagnetic field surrounding the physical body.

D

Divine Mother: also referred to as Kundalini can be interpreted as the force which enables life.

E

Easy Pose: often used in many types of yoga to refer to a relaxed crossed-leg siting potion with straight spine.

I

Intuition: '…natural ability or power that makes it possible to know something without any proof or evidence...' I like to think it is a human superpower we unlearned how to use. Like trusting a medium to tell your fortune for the near future. The medium uses intuition to interpret and deliver the messages it receives for you, that is a person who exercises intuition like a muscle to be able to offer the best accuracy. Is not relevant if what intuition taps into is via spirits or 'quantic realities', what is relevant is that we all have it, and it takes practise to learn to re-connect with the 'signs of the world' as Paulo Coelho often mentions. Another part of intuition is trust, in a time where anyone with access to your Facebook activity can easily conjure up a prediction that touches your heart makes it all more difficult. I found I can amplify my intuition by just improving my focus through meditation, no hocus-pocus, just a standard clearing out of the 'chatty mind' and its distractions.

J

Japji: Japji Sahib, sacred hymn said to be composed by Guru Nanak Dev Ji, the founder of the Sikh faith. Is also a text which is often recited during kundalini *Sadhana* practice early in the morning. Many Sikh *mantras* and language were incorporated by Yogi Bhajan when designing the Kundalini practise for the Western folk. However is interesting to note that the Sikh tradition itself does not practise a form of yoga or another per se. In both traditions the ancient Sikh faith and the modern Kundalini practice the entire *Japji* is recited during morning meditation (Sadhana).

K

Kriya: generally refers to a sequence of kundalini exercises designed to prepare the body for a specific meditation or effect, i.e. improve kidney function, release stress, sleep better, etc. Kundalini exercises much like other yoga practices can be either by a pose, breath or hand position, also known respectively as *asanas*, pranayama and *mudras*.

Kundalini: in this publication it generally refers to the yoga practice designed by Yogi Bhajan in the 60s whilst living in the United States. Kundalini in other contexts can also allure to the core energy which propels life in our human body. Often in Kundalini yoga you hear about 'kundalini rising' which is the believe once an yogi has cleared all its *chakras* this energy is able to free flow from the base of the spine up to the head, thus rising.

L

Long Time Sun Shine song: Another curious factoid is that sometime during 60s-70s 'May the Long Time Sun Shine Upon You' became a closing prayer-song for Kundalini yoga. What is less known is this chant was originally the last part of the track 'A Very Cellular Song' from 'The Hangman's Beautiful Daughter' 2005 album by the Scottish-based folk band, Incredible String Band (ISB). Written by one of the band's founders, Mike Heron, who funny enough is neither a Sikh or an yogi. There are even some claims it has ancient Celtic roots. What is certain is that it is special. The Kundalini excerpt of that song is:

'May the long-time sun shine upon you,
all love surround you
and the pure light within you,
guide your way on'

M

Mantra: in many types of yoga is referred to as a series of prayers or sometimes just short words repeated many times in combination with a breath exercise *(pranayama)* or position *(asana)*.

Mudras: in many types of yoga is referred to specific hand positions used in combination with dynamic or static exercises or meditations.

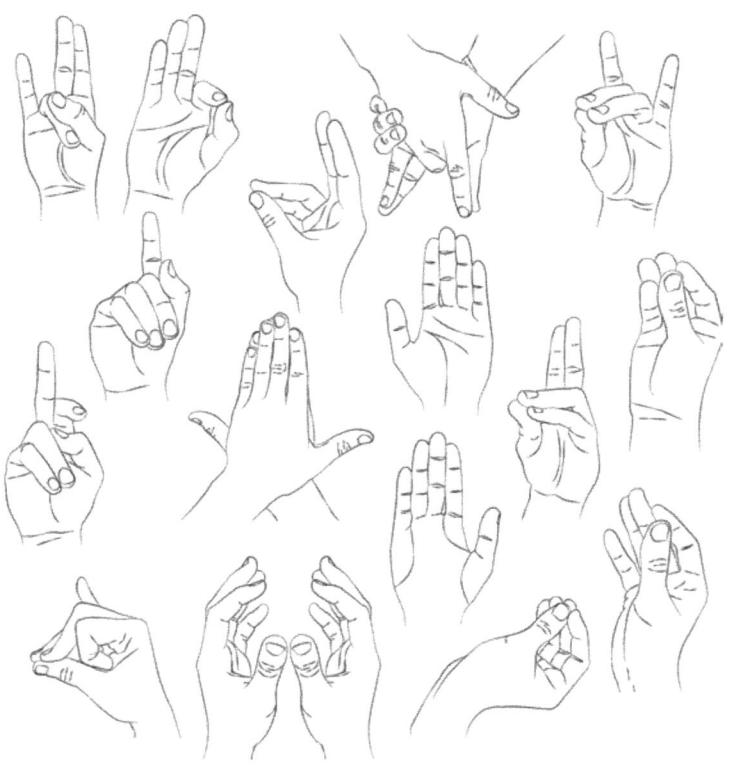

Mulah Bandah: in many types of yoga is referred to as *root lock* a series of inner muscles from your sexual organs area to the upper abdomen. One is often asked to hold (contract) the 'mulah bandah' when doing exercises for the core and during the hold of a long breath of exhale to maximise the effect of the exercise or meditation.

N

Neck Lock: holding your chin slightly tucked in and shoulders down.

P

Prana, Pranee, Pranayama: from Sanskrit meaning 'life-force', this term is used in Hinduism and is also typically used in yoga practices, martial arts and Indian medicine. Prana is also referred to as the universal source of breath, literally meaning life energy, your source of divine energy.

R

Reiki: is an original method of healing, developed by Mikao Usui in Japan early in the 20th century, which is activated literally by intention. It works on every level, not just the physical and also is often referred to as 'energy transmission'.

Root lock: same as *Mulah Bandah.*

S

Sat Nam: is a chant often used in Sikh practices and Kundalini yoga, from Sanskrit meaning 'My name is Truth'. I found that this is also used as a greeting when meeting people of such practices whilst holding their gaze gently almost as a gesture of trust.

Satsang: a 'getting together of good people' generally of the same spiritual framework. In Sanskrit reads as: sat=truth and sang=company. In yoga groups or events translates as a medium for sharing of workshops, events and community related activities of a specific yoga practice.

Sitali breath: said to be able to cool down the body's temperature consists of a breathing technique where one slowly inhales air with a curled tongue, consciously expanding the belly and raising the upper thorax as it gets filled. The curled tongue consists of sticking it out and curling it so that the sides touch each other. The lips are closed around the tongue in a circular shape so that the air passes through the hole and not around. This may occasionally produce a hissing or whistling sound. The exhale happens through the nose which in non-kundalini practices is referred to as Ujjayi breath.

Stretch pose: unlike other asanas which are practiced amongst a variety of yoga traditions, this pose is unique to Kundalini yoga. Amongst many things it requires that after lying down one lifts legs, arms and legs at 6 inches from the floor, normally holding it for at least 3 minutes.

Sun salutations: consists of a series of asanas that literally make you bow to the 'sun'. This sequence is thought to have been likely developed in modern times. Coming back from sun salutations to the standing position involves passing through plank and the famous yoga push-up 'chaturanga'

T

Third eye: I find that often you are asked to close your eyes and 'look' between your eyebrows to stimulate this ethereal location in the body, 6th chakra. This is often associated with intuition.

W

White Tantric Yoga: To start with this is not the sex yoga which most people think of when hearing the word 'tantra'. It is a fair misconception as even in the East where it was born, 'tantra' has a variety of definitions mostly born out of oral-tradition. Tan is a Sanskrit root which signifies 'expansion', and Tra signifies 'liberation', being free. So in many aspects the term itself simply means largely 'being happy'. So without offending any religious studies scholars and for the purpose of this publication for Kundalini White Tantric refers to the events Kundalini folk promote all over the world. It entails a full day of sets of 32 to 64 minutes positions, which may include static movements, breathing techniques, etc. The catch here is that you do it with a partner. Traditionally they prefer is male and female to work with something called the Z energy. But what starts a bit odd as most sets consist of 'open eye meditation', that is looking at your partner's eye through the duration of the sets, ends up being a very freeing experience. I remember for months after that event I just held my gaze a little better when looking at someone's eyes for the first time and started noticing that at least in the big city people rarely looked at each other's eyes anymore.

Y

Yoga: in the western is referred to the many meditative practices originated in what is now known as India. Generally the yoga traditions steam from the Buddhist spiritual practices but there are other forms. Tantra for instance is known in India by many different names and origins. For example Kundalini as taught by Yogi Bhajan was designed by himself to combine dynamic target sets of exercises aligned with the spiritual Sikh tradition which is different from Buddhism although it uses many asanas and breathing techniques derived from that tradition. Another popular one this days and also one of my favourites in Vinyasa flow, which combines many of the Hatha yogic traditions into a non-dogmatic practice where the teacher can add their own flavour into the mix. This Vinyasa practise not only became very popular because of its dynamic sets but also because it does not require a spiritual 'conversion' to advance as a student, such as taking a spiritual name and completely changing life-style.

ABOUT THE AUTHOR

Born in Brazil via California and a 'mezzo Italiana',
Paolla is a writer who has made London her home
and amongst many things she loves cats,
open water swimming, spreadsheets,
falling asleep just at the right spot,
pretending she still is a professional dancer
at Pineapple Studios' classes
and the occasional Hobnob.

SPECIAL THANK YOU

to all of those friends and family
who helped me get here,
including the invisible ones,
you know who you are

Luna who melted my heart ♥

Left to right: Cook and Luna (2013-2014)

and my personal Zen master, Cook,
who frequently woke me up at 4am
for meditation followed by a writing session
during the creation of this book…

and for the survivour inside
who has protected the softer part of me until
we were both ready to let go,
thank you

I now release you with
love and eternal gratitude
for bringing me this far

You were awesome!

I Bastioni, Anghiari,Tuscany - 2006

CPSIA information can be obtained
at www.ICGtesting.com
Printed in the USA
LVHW05s1547060518
576190LV00034B/1353/P

9 780957 534179